TOXIC WORKPLACE

Identification, Prevention and Healing

DR. RAVINDRAN.K.A.

GUIDED SELF PUBLISHING (I) LLP

ISBN NO. 9789314100293

MRP Rs.299/- 9.99 $

Book Cover by Guided Self Publishing (I) LLP

Published by Guided Self Publishing (I) LLP, Sohna Haryana

Print & Distributed by Advika Book Mart

First edition 2024

Dedication

To my family, whose unwavering love and support have been my foundation and inspiration.

To my previous bosses, teachers and who have imparted invaluable wisdom and guidance, shaping my journey and understanding of leadership and workplace culture.

To all the dedicated professionals striving to create healthier, more positive workplaces.

And to every employee who has ever felt the weight of a toxic work environment—may this book be a beacon of hope and a guide to a brighter, more fulfilling future.

With gratitude and hope,

Dr. Ravindran.K.A.
HR Management Professional
Transformation Coach & Author

Content

Advance Praise for the Book

Dr. Ravindran.K.A.'s book, **'Toxic Workplace: Identification, Prevention and Healing,'** is a beacon of hope for organisations grappling with workplace toxicity. With compassion and expertise, Dr.Ravindran delves into the heart of the issue, offering practical solutions that empower both employees and leaders.

The book masterfully dissects the various forms of toxicity—subtle or overt—that poison work environments. Dr Ravindran's insights are backed by real-world examples, making them relatable and actionable. From passive aggression to outright bullying, he sheds light on the impact of toxic behaviour and its ripple effects.

What sets this book apart is its emphasis on prevention. Dr. Ravindran doesn't merely diagnose the problem; he prescribes remedies. Chapters on effective communication, policy implementation, and fostering a positive culture provide a roadmap for transformation.

As a professional, I found 'Toxic Workplace' invaluable. It equips us with tools to create workplaces where employees thrive, productivity soars, and turnover rates plummet. Dr. Ravindran's passion for healing toxic environments shines through every page.

Thank you, Dr. Ravindran, for championing healthier workplaces. Your book is a catalyst for positive change.

Bob. Seshadri
Author
Retired Automobile Management Professional

Catalyst for creating a healthier and more productive work environment for all

As a senior executive with decades of experience in navigating complex landscapes of corporate environments, I am honoured to be a recipient of a copy of this book, **Toxic Workplace: Identification, Prevention and Healing** and provide my views on the same.

In an era where the pace and pressures of work can often lead to unhealthy dynamics, this book provides practical guidance to identify, prevent and heal Toxicity. From the first page to the last, this comprehensive guide lays out a clear path for recognising and addressing workplace toxicity in its many forms. The profound impacts of toxic environments affecting employee well-being and organisational success are well-documented,

High turnover rates, diminished productivity, and escalating healthcare costs are just a few of the harmful effects that stem from a toxic workplace. **This book explores deep into the early signs of toxicity, offering practical insights and actionable strategies for transformation**.

By providing real-world examples and case studies, Dr Ravindran has proved how these strategies have successfully turned around toxic work environments. The data charts and graphs further highlight the critical importance and effectiveness of these initiatives.

As you turn these pages, you will find valuable tools and knowledge to foster a positive, respectful, and empowering workplace culture. It is my sincere belief that, armed with the insights from this book, we can transform our workplaces into havens of engagement, innovation, and mutual respect.

Whether you are a business leader, manager, HR professional, or an employee striving to make a difference, this book is a treasure trove of guidance and inspiration.

May this book become the catalyst for positive change in your organization, to create healthier and more productive work environments for all.

Sincerely,

Gita Ramachandran

Retired Senior Executive from Bharat Petroleum

Founder of Gita's Gyan Academy

Author, Mentor, Digital Success and Leadership and Life-skills Coach

https://gitaramachandran.com

'Toxic Workplace: Identification, Prevention and Healing' is a vital resource for anyone committed to transforming their work environment. This book provides clear, actionable strategies for identifying and addressing workplace toxicity, helping to foster a culture of respect and productivity.

With practical insights and real-world examples, it equips readers with the tools needed to create healthy, thriving workplaces.

A must-read for leaders, managers, and employees alike, it inspires and guides the journey towards a more positive organisational culture.

Hemant Nag
Delivery Head @ Bacancy, Ahmedabad &
Author

"Great things are done by a series of small things brought together - Vincent Van Gogh"

As a team the only way to build a great place can be achieved through hard work, being humble, kind and nice to each other to achieve business goals. This book gives the right guidelines to create a happy and healthier work environment. It is a must-read book!!!.

Saheesh Mohandas
Entrepreneur,
Business Management Consultant

This book is like a guiding light for people who are stuck in a bad work environment. The author shares inspiring stories in a way that's easy to relate to. It shows how harmful toxic workplaces can be and helps you take back control and make things better for yourself.

Dinesh Divekar
Business Mentor, Consultant & Trainer

Acknowledgements

Writing ***"Toxic Workplace: Identification, Prevention and Healing"*** has been a deeply rewarding journey, and it would not have been possible without the support, encouragement and contributions of many individuals.

First and foremost, I would like to express my heartfelt gratitude to my family for their unwavering support and patience throughout this process. Your love and understanding have been my anchor, and I am eternally grateful for your belief in me.

I extend my sincere thanks to my colleagues/ex-colleagues and friends who offered their invaluable insights and experiences, enriching the content of this book with real-world perspectives. Your stories, both triumphant and challenging, have provided a solid foundation for the practical advice and strategies presented here.

A special thank you goes to the many professionals and organizations who participated in interviews, surveys and case studies. Your willingness to share your time and expertise has been instrumental in bringing this book to life. Your contributions have helped ensure that the strategies discussed are not only theoretically sound but also practically viable.

I am deeply grateful to my editor, whose keen eye and thoughtful feedback have greatly enhanced the clarity and coherence of this book. Your dedication and meticulous attention to detail have been invaluable.

I also wish to acknowledge the researchers and thought leaders whose work has inspired and informed this book. The wealth of knowledge and research available on workplace culture, psychology and organizational behaviour has been a rich resource that has greatly influenced my thinking and writing.

To my publisher, thank you for believing in this project and providing the platform to share these insights with a wider audience. Your support and professionalism have been crucial in bringing this book to fruition.

Finally, I want to thank the readers. Your commitment to improving workplace culture and your willingness to engage with these ideas are what make this endeavour worthwhile. I hope this book provides you with the tools and inspiration needed to create healthier, more productive work environments.

Thank you all for your contributions, support and encouragement. Together, we can make a meaningful difference in the way we work and interact within our professional lives.

With deep appreciation,

Dr.Ravindran.K.A.
HR Management Professional,
Transformation Coach & Author

Foreword

In the ever-evolving landscape of today's workplace, the importance of a healthy and supportive work environment cannot be overstated. It is within this context that I am honoured to introduce ***"Toxic Workplace: Identification, Prevention and Healing"*** a vital resource for anyone committed to creating and maintaining a positive workplace culture.

Workplace toxicity is a silent but powerful force that can undermine even the most well-intentioned organizations. It erodes trust, stifles innovation, and can lead to a cascade of negative outcomes, from high turnover and absenteeism to diminished morale and productivity. Yet, despite its pervasive impact, toxicity is often overlooked or misunderstood.

This book is a clarion call to acknowledge and address the realities of workplace toxicity. It provides a comprehensive guide to recognizing the signs of a toxic environment and offers practical, actionable strategies for transforming it. The authors have drawn upon a wealth of research, case studies and real-world examples to illustrate the profound effects of toxicity and the steps that can be taken to counteract it.

One of the book's greatest strengths lies in its accessibility. The authors have distilled complex concepts into clear, straightforward language, making it an invaluable tool for leaders, managers, HR professionals and employees alike. Whether you are seeking to understand the root causes of toxicity, develop effective conflict resolution skills or implement inclusive policies and training programs, this book offers a roadmap for change.

Moreover, the emphasis on data-driven insights and visual aids provides readers with the tools to measure progress and make informed decisions. The inclusion of diverse case studies showcases successful transformations, proving that positive change is not only possible but also sustainable.

In a world where the pressures of work can often feel overwhelming, this book serves as both a guide and an inspiration. It reminds us that creating a positive workplace is not a one-time effort but an ongoing journey that requires dedication, empathy and a willingness to listen and learn.

As you embark on this journey through the pages of ***"Toxic Workplace: Identification, Prevention and Healing",*** I encourage you to embrace the principles and practices outlined within. By doing so, you will be taking crucial steps towards fostering an environment where every employee feels valued, respected and empowered to contribute their best work.

Let us commit to building workplaces that are not only free of toxicity but are also beacons of positivity, collaboration and innovation. Together, we can create a future where work is a source of fulfillment and growth for all.

With optimism and determination,

Dr. S.Y. Siddiqui
Former ED HR/COO (HR/ FIN./IT/Legal) /
Chief Mentor & Executive Advisor
Maruti Suzuki

Preface

Welcome to "Toxic Workplace: Identification, Prevention and Healing". This book is designed to serve as a comprehensive guide for recognizing, addressing and ultimately transforming toxic work environments into healthy, productive spaces. In today's fast-paced and often high-stress work culture, it's more important than ever to create workplaces where employees feel valued, respected and empowered.

Workplace toxicity can take many forms, from indirect undermining and passive aggression to obvious bullying and harassment. The impact of such toxicity is profound, affecting not only the well-being of individual employees but also the overall health and success of the organization. High turnover rates, decreased productivity and increased healthcare costs are just a few of the adverse outcomes that can result from a toxic work environment.

In this book, we explore deep into the many facets of workplace toxicity. From identifying the early signs of negative attitudes and behaviours to understanding the broader implications on organizational success, each chapter provides practical insights and actionable strategies. You'll learn how to conduct effective employee surveys, establish clear policies and procedures and promote open communication and training programs that foster a positive workplace culture.

Real-world examples and case studies illustrate the transformative power of these strategies, showing how organizations have successfully turned around toxic environments. Visual aids, such as data charts and graphs, help to underscore the importance of these initiatives and track their effectiveness over time.

Our goal is to equip you with the tools and knowledge needed to create a workplace where everyone can thrive. Whether you're a business leader, manager, HR professional or an employee looking to make a difference, this book offers valuable guidance and inspiration.

Together, we can build workplaces that are not just free of toxicity, but also places of engagement, innovation and mutual respect. Let's embark on this journey to create healthier, more productive work environments for all.

Thank you for joining us on this important mission.

Sincerely,
Dr. Ravindran. K.A.
HR Management Professional,
Transformation Coach & Author

Introduction

Welcome, exhausted traveller, to the land of **Toxic Workplace**. This is not just any workplace; it's a web of stress, negativity and dysfunction that can drain your energy and sap your enthusiasm. But fear not, for within these pages, you will find the tools, insights and strategies to navigate this unfaithful terrain and emerge stronger, wiser and more resilient than ever before.

Picture this: you walk into the office each day, shoulders hunched and heart heavy. The air is thick with tension and you can practically taste the bitterness lingering in every interaction. Maybe it's the relentless micromanagement, the constant backstabbing or the soul-crushing lack of appreciation. Whatever the cause, you know deep down that this is not how work should be.

But here's the thing: you are not alone. According to a recent study by the Harvard Business Review, a staggering 76% of employees report experiencing some form of toxicity in their workplace. That's three out of every four workers who are grappling with the same challenges, facing the same battles, and dreaming of a better tomorrow.

So, what exactly is a toxic workplace? It's more than just a bad boss or a difficult coworker. It's an environment where negativity reigns supreme, where trust is in short supply and where even the most resilient souls can find themselves on the brink of burnout. It's a place where gossip spreads like wildfire, where groups form and groups clash and where the pursuit of success comes at the expense of basic human decency.

But here's the good news: toxicity is not inevitable and change is possible. In fact, organizations that ***prioritize employee well-being and foster a culture of respect and collaboration are not only more productive and profitable but also more resilient in the face of adversity.*** Consider the case of Company X (you read as an example company throughout the book) a once-struggling startup that transformed itself into a thriving industry leader by prioritizing transparency, empathy and open communication. By investing ***in employee training, implementing clear policies against harassment and discrimination and cultivating a sense of belonging***

and purpose, Company* X *not only reduced turnover and absenteeism but also attracted top talent and earned the loyalty of its customers.

So, how can you recognize the signs of toxicity in your own workplace? It's not always easy, but there are some significant indicators to watch out for. *Are you constantly on edge, fearing interactions with certain colleagues or superiors? Do you find yourself feeling drained and demoralized at the end of each day? Are you witnessing patterns of bullying, harassment or discrimination that go unchecked or even overlooked by those in power?* These are just a few of the red flags that may signal the presence of toxicity in your midst.

But fear not - knowledge is power and armed with the right insights and strategies, you can reclaim your agency and chart a course towards a brighter future. In the chapters that follow, we'll explore deeper into the root causes of toxicity, explore the various forms it can take, and offer practical tips and techniques for addressing and overcoming dysfunction in your workplace. From setting boundaries and advocating for yourself to fostering a culture of respect and resilience, we'll cover it all, drawing on the latest research, real-world examples and the collective wisdom of those who have walked this path before.

So, whether you're a seasoned professional navigating the ups and downs of corporate life or a recent graduate just dipping your toes into the workforce, I invite you to join me on this journey. Together, we'll shine a light into the darkest corners of the Toxic Workplace, uncovering hidden truths, dispelling myths, and paving the way for a brighter tomorrow. It won't be easy, and the road may be long, but remember: you are not alone and the power to change lies within each and every one of us. So let's roll up our sleeves, sharpen our swords and march forward with courage and conviction. The battle against toxicity begins now, and victory is within reach.

Chapter 1

Understanding Toxicity in the Workplace

Introduction

Imagine waking up each day fearing going to work. You step into the office and a wave of tension hits you. Conversations are filled with whispers and negativity. Your heart races as you check your email, expecting criticism or unreasonable demands. This scenario is all too common in toxic workplaces.

Toxic workplaces are more than just places where people have bad days. They are environments where negativity and dysfunction thrive, affecting everyone's well-being and productivity. In this chapter, we will explore what makes a workplace toxic, how to recognize it and why addressing these issues is crucial.

Defining a Toxic Workplace

A toxic workplace is one where negative behaviours and poor management practices create a harmful environment. It's a place where employees feel undervalued, unsupported and even harassed. This constant stress and negativity can take a severe toll on mental, emotional and physical health.

Key Characteristics of a Toxic Workplace

1. *Poor Leadership*: Leaders who are abusive, micromanaging or indifferent to employee well-being.

2. *Lack of Communication*: Important information is often withheld and transparency is non-existent.

3. *High-Stress Levels*: Unreasonable deadlines, excessive workloads/wrong work assignments and no respect for work-life balance.

4. *Negative Environment*: Gossip, bullying and cliques dominate the culture.

5. *Low Morale*: Employees feel demotivated, unappreciated and disconnected from their work.

Recognizing the Signs

Identifying a toxic workplace is the first step toward addressing the problem. Here are some signs to watch out for:

1. High Turnover Rates

A high turnover rate is a clear indicator of a toxic workplace. When employees are constantly leaving, it often signals that the environment is unbearable. According to a study by the Work Institute, 22% of employees leave their jobs due to toxic work cultures.

2. Frequent Absenteeism

Employees in toxic workplaces tend to call in sick more often. This isn't just about physical illness but also mental health issues like stress and anxiety.

3. Low Productivity

Toxic environments kill motivation. When employees are stressed or unhappy, their productivity suffers. A Gallup study found that disengaged employees have 37% higher absenteeism, 18% lower productivity and 15% lower profitability.

4. Negative Communication Patterns

In toxic workplaces, communication is often negative. This includes gossip, backstabbing and a lack of constructive feedback. Employees may feel they cannot speak up without facing repercussions.

5. Lack of Trust

Trust is the foundation of a healthy workplace. In toxic environments, trust is eroded through inconsistent policies, favouritism and broken promises.

The Impact of Toxicity

The effects of a toxic workplace extend beyond the employees—they impact the entire organization.

1. Employee Health

Stress is a major factor in many health issues, from heart disease to depression. The American Psychological Association reports that workplace stress costs the U.S. economy over $500 billion annually and is linked to 120,000 deaths each year.

2. Company Pcrformancc

Toxic workplaces are bad for business. Low morale leads to high turnover and low productivity, affecting the bottom line.

A study by the Queens School of Business and the Gallup Organization found that disengaged workers had 37% higher absenteeism, 49% more accidents and 60% more errors and defects.

3. Reputation

Word spreads quickly about toxic workplaces. This can make it difficult to attract top talent. A Glassdoor survey found that 77% of job seekers consider a company's culture before applying for a job.

Real-Life Example: A famous Car Rental Company's Toxic Culture

In 2017, a popular car rental company faced a major crisis due to its toxic work culture. Reports of harassment, discrimination and unethical behaviour surfaced, leading to a public relations nightmare. The company lost significant talent, faced lawsuits and saw a drop in user trust. This example highlights how a toxic workplace can damage even the most successful companies.

Best Practices for Recognizing and Addressing Toxicity

1. Conduct Regular Surveys

Regularly ask employees for their feedback on the work environment. Anonymous surveys can help identify issues that might not be visible at first glance. Tools like SurveyMonkey or Google Forms are effective for this purpose.

2. Promote Open Communication

Encourage an open-door policy where employees feel safe to voice their concerns without fear of retaliation. Regular team meetings and one-on-ones can foster this environment.

3. Implement Clear Policies

Have clear, well-communicated policies against bullying, harassment and discrimination. Ensure there are defined procedures for reporting and addressing such issues.

4. Provide Support Resources

Offer resources like counselling services, stress management workshops and wellness programs. These can help employees manage stress and feel valued by their employers.

5. Lead by Example

Leaders should model the behaviour they expect from their team. This means being transparent, showing empathy and promoting a positive work culture.

Visualizing the Data

Visual aids can help illustrate the impact of toxic workplaces. Below are some examples:

High Turnover Rates

A chart comparing turnover rates in toxic versus healthy workplaces can be eye-opening. For instance, companies with toxic cultures may see turnover rates of 30-40%, compared to 10-15% in healthier environments.

Employee Absenteeism

A graph comparing absenteeism rates can highlight blunt differences. Toxic workplaces might see absenteeism rates of 15-20%, while healthy workplaces maintain rates around 5-7%.

Productivity Levels

A graph showing productivity metrics can emphasize the financial impact. Disengaged employees could lead to a 15-20% drop in productivity compared to engaged employees.

Conclusion

Understanding what makes a workplace toxic is crucial for anyone looking to improve their work environment. Toxicity isn't just about a bad day or a tough project; it's a persistent, damaging atmosphere that affects everyone. By recognizing the signs, understanding the impacts and implementing the best practices, we can start to turn the tide.

As you move forward, remember that change starts with awareness. By being vigilant and proactive, you can help create a healthier, more positive work environment for yourself and your colleagues. The journey to a better workplace begins with understanding and from here, we will explore the tools and strategies needed to navigate and transform even the most toxic of workplaces.

Action Steps

1. Start with Self-Assessment: Reflect on your work environment. Identify any signs of toxicity.

2. Open Dialogue: Initiate conversations with colleagues to share observations and concerns.

3. Seek Support: Look for resources within your organization or seek external advice from HR professionals or counsellors.

4. Take Small Steps: Implement small changes that can lead to bigger shifts in culture, such as promoting kindness and collaboration in daily interactions.

Remember, creating a positive work environment is a collective effort. Every small step counts towards building a healthier, happier workplace. Let's take those steps together.

Chapter 2

The Effects of Toxicity on Individuals and Organizations

Introduction

Toxic workplaces do more than just make you dread going to work. They create a ripple effect that can impact every aspect of both personal and professional life. Understanding these effects is crucial for making the case for change. In this chapter, we will explore how toxicity in the workplace affects individuals and organizations. We will delve into the mental, physical and emotional toll it takes on employees, as well as the financial and operational impact on businesses.

The Toll on Individuals

Mental Health

The mental health of employees is often the first casualty in a toxic workplace. Constant stress and negativity can lead to anxiety, depression and burnout. According to the American Institute of Stress, work-related stress is a leading cause of mental health issues, with 83% of US workers suffering from work-related stress.

Example:

Consider Ms. X, a marketing manager at a tech firm. Her boss frequently belittles her in meetings and sets unrealistic deadlines. Over time, Ms.X begins to feel anxious and starts doubting her abilities. Her sleep suffers and she becomes irritable at home, affecting her family life as well.

Physical Health

The physical effects of a toxic workplace are just as concerning. Stress can lead to a range of health problems, including headaches, high blood pressure, heart disease and weakened immune systems. The World Health Organization estimates that long working hours are responsible for 745,000 deaths from stroke and ischemic heart disease annually. https://www.who.int/news/item/17-05-2021-long-working-hours-increasing-deaths-from-heart-disease-and-stroke-who-ilo

Example:

Mr. Y, a software developer, works in a high-stress environment where he is constantly worried about job security. He starts experiencing chronic headaches and high blood pressure. His doctor attributes these symptoms to his stressful work conditions.

Emotional Well-being

Emotionally, toxic workplaces can be draining. They often lead to feelings of hopelessness, frustration and helplessness. Employees might feel trapped, unable to see a way out or a path to improvement.

Example:

Ms. Z, an administrative assistant, feels emotionally drained every day. Her coworkers often gossip about her, and she feels isolated. This constant emotional strain makes it hard for her to stay positive or motivated.

The Impact on Organizations

Reduced Productivity

A toxic workplace is a productivity killer. Employees who are stressed, demotivated or unwell cannot perform at their best. This drop in productivity can significantly impact the bottom line. According to a Gallup poll, disengaged employees cost U.S. companies up to $550 billion annually in lost productivity.

Example:

A sales team in a toxic environment misses targets regularly. The constant pressure and lack of support demoralize the team, leading to lower sales and lost revenue.

High Turnover Rates

High turnover is a common consequence of a toxic workplace. When employees leave frequently, it disrupts operations and incurs high recruitment and training costs. The Society for Human Resource Management (SHRM) estimates that the average cost to replace an employee is six to nine months' salary.

Example:

A consulting firm experiences high turnover due to a toxic culture. The constant influx of new employees who need to be trained affects the company's ability to maintain high-quality client service.

Increased Absenteeism

Employees in toxic workplaces are more likely to call in sick. This absenteeism can disrupt workflows and increase the burden on other employees, creating a vicious cycle and also impacting productivity and revenues. The Centers for Disease Control and Prevention (CDC) reports that absenteeism costs employers $225.8 billion annually.

https://www.cdcfoundation.org/pr/2015/worker-illness-and-injury-costs-us-employers-225-billion-annually#:~:text=The%20Centers%20for%20Disease%20Control,among%20employers%20of%20all%20sizes.

Example:

In a manufacturing company, high levels of absenteeism due to stress and burnout lead to missed production targets and increased overtime costs.

Poor Reputation

Companies with toxic cultures quickly gain a bad reputation. This can make it difficult to attract top talent and can also affect relationships with clients and partners. A Glassdoor survey found that 77% of job seekers consider a company's culture before applying for a job.

Example:

A well-known fashion retailer struggles to hire new talent due to its reputation for having a toxic work environment. Negative reviews on job sites deter potential candidates.

Real-World Case: The Downfall of M/s Enron

The collapse of M/s Enron is a textbook example of how a toxic culture can destroy a company. Enron's culture was marked by unethical behaviour, intense pressure to meet unrealistic targets and a lack of accountability. This toxic environment led to fraudulent activities and ultimately the company's downfall, affecting thousands of employees and investors.

https://www.linkedin.com/pulse/organizational-culture-how-enron-did-wrong-jason-martin-mba

Best Practices to Mitigate Toxicity

Foster Open Communication

Open communication is crucial for addressing and preventing toxicity. Employees should feel safe to express concerns without fear of retaliation. Regular town hall meetings, suggestion boxes and anonymous surveys can help.

Example:

A company implemented weekly team check-ins where employees could voice concerns. This practice led to improved morale and better team cohesion.

Promote Work-Life Balance

Encouraging a healthy work-life balance can reduce stress and improve overall well-being. Flexible working hours, remote work options and ensuring employees take their leave can help.

Example:

A finance firm introduced flexible working hours and saw a significant drop in employee burnout rates. Productivity and job satisfaction improved as a result.

Recognize and Reward Employees

Recognition and rewards can boost morale and motivate employees. Regularly acknowledging hard work and providing incentives can create a positive work environment.

Example:

A retail company implemented an employee of the month program. This simple act of recognition improved morale and encouraged a positive, supportive work culture.

Provide Professional Career Development Opportunities

Investing in employees' growth shows that the company values them. Offering training programs, workshops and career advancement opportunities can help retain talent and reduce employee turnover.

Example:

A marketing agency offered regular training sessions on the latest industry trends. Employees felt more valued and stayed longer with the company.

Visualizing the Data

To illustrate the impact of toxic workplaces, visual data can be very effective. Here are some examples:

Mental Health Impact

A chart can show the percentage of employees reporting stress, anxiety and depression in toxic versus healthy workplaces. For instance, 60% in toxic environments versus 20% in healthy ones.

Turnover Rates

A graph comparing turnover rates over five years in companies with toxic and healthy cultures can highlight the stark differences.

Productivity Metrics

A graph showing productivity levels in different departments before and after addressing workplace toxicity can demonstrate the financial benefits of a healthy work environment.

Conclusion

The effects of a toxic workplace are far-reaching and harmful, impacting both individuals and organizations. Understanding these effects is the first step towards making meaningful changes. By recognizing the signs and implementing best practices, companies can create a healthier, more productive work environment.

Creating a positive workplace culture is not just about avoiding negative outcomes. It's about fostering a space where employees can prosper, feel valued and contribute to the company's success. In the next chapters, we will explore actionable strategies and real-world examples to help transform toxic workplaces into healthy, flourishing environments. Let's take the next step together in building better workplaces for everyone.

Chapter 3

Identifying Toxicity in Your Workplace

Introduction

Toxicity in the workplace can silently erode morale, reduce productivity and increase turnover. It's crucial to recognize the signs early and address them promptly to foster a healthier work environment. In this chapter, we will explore how to identify toxicity in your workplace, understand its impact and implement best practices to address and prevent it.

Recognizing the Signs of Workplace Toxicity

Negative Attitudes and Behaviors

One of the most obvious signs of a toxic workplace is the prevalence of negative attitudes and behaviours. This can manifest as consistent negativity, hostility or unprofessional behaviour among employees.

Example:

An employee who constantly complains and criticizes others without constructive feedback or displays a lack of respect towards colleagues and management may be contributing to a toxic environment.

High Turnover Rates

A high turnover rate is often a red flag indicating underlying issues within the workplace. Employees tend to leave toxic environments in search of healthier, more supportive workplaces.

Data:

According to the Work Institute's Retention Report, the cost of turnover can be as high as 33% of an employee's annual salary, making it a costly issue for organizations.

https://info.workinstitute.com/hubfs/2022%20Retention%20Report/2022%20Retention%20Report%20-%20Work%20Institute.pdf

Increased Absenteeism

Frequent absenteeism can be a symptom of a toxic work environment. Employees may take more sick days or personal time off to avoid a hostile or stressful workplace.

Example:

If an employee who previously had good attendance starts taking frequent sick days, it might be worth investigating whether workplace toxicity is a contributing factor.

Poor Communication

In a toxic workplace, communication often breaks down. This can include a lack of transparency from management, ineffective or hostile communication among team members and a general atmosphere of mistrust.

Example:

Team meetings that are consistently unproductive, filled with blame-shifting, or where employees feel afraid to speak up, can be a sign of poor communication stemming from a toxic culture.

Impact of Toxicity on the Organization

Decreased Productivity

Toxic behaviours and attitudes can significantly reduce overall productivity. Employees who are unhappy or stressed are less likely to perform at their best and may be less willing to go above and beyond in their roles.

Data:

A study by the Harvard Business Review found that workplace toxicity can lead to a 40% decline in employee productivity.

https://www.hbs.edu/ris/Publication%20Files/16-057_d45c0b4f-fa19-49de-8f1b-4b12fe054fea.pdf

Lower Employee Engagement

Employee engagement suffers in a toxic environment. Engaged employees are enthusiastic and committed to their work, but toxicity can erode this engagement, leading to disengagement and apathy.

Example:

In a company where gossip and backstabbing are common, employees are less likely to feel valued or motivated, leading to lower levels of engagement and morale.

Increased Healthcare Costs

Workplace toxicity can also contribute to increased healthcare costs due to stress-related illnesses. Chronic stress from a toxic environment can lead to both mental and physical health issues.

Data:

The American Psychological Association estimates that workplace stress costs the U.S. economy more than $500 billion annually in lost productivity and increased healthcare costs.

https://www.stress.org/workplace-stress

Best Practices for Identifying and Addressing Toxicity

Conduct Regular Employee Surveys

Regularly surveying employees can help identify issues related to workplace toxicity. Surveys should include questions about job satisfaction, workplace culture and any specific issues employees may be facing.

Example:

A company conducts quarterly anonymous surveys to gauge employee satisfaction and identify potential areas of concern.

The feedback is used to implement changes and address issues before they escalate.

Establish Clear Policies and Procedures

Having clear policies and procedures in place can help prevent and address toxic behaviours. These should include codes of conduct, anti-harassment policies and clear procedures for reporting and addressing grievances.

Example:

A healthcare organization implements a zero-tolerance policy for bullying and harassment, along with a confidential reporting system to ensure employees feel safe coming forward with concerns.

Promote Open Communication

Encouraging open and honest communication can help identify and resolve issues before they contribute to a toxic environment. This includes regular one-on-one meetings, team meetings and an open-door policy with management.

Example:

A financial services firm holds monthly town hall meetings where employees can anonymously submit questions or concerns to be addressed by senior management. This practice promotes transparency and trust within the organization.

Facilitate Training and Development

Offering training and development programs can equip employees and managers with the skills needed to foster a positive workplace culture. This includes training on conflict resolution, communication skills and leadership development.

Example:

A manufacturing company offers workshops on effective communication and conflict resolution to all employees, helping to build a more respectful and collaborative workplace.

Monitor and Address Workplace Dynamics

Regularly monitoring workplace dynamics can help identify potential sources of toxicity. This includes observing interactions between employees, team dynamics and overall workplace atmosphere.

Example:

A retail company conducts periodic reviews of team dynamics and uses the findings to implement team-building activities and address any issues that may arise.

Case Study: Turn Around a Toxic Workplace

The Situation

A mid-sized marketing firm was experiencing high turnover, low employee morale and frequent conflicts among team members. Employee surveys revealed widespread dissatisfaction with management and a lack of trust within the organization.

The Approach

1. Leadership Change: The company brought in a new CEO with a strong commitment to improving workplace culture.

2. Policy Overhaul: The new leadership implemented clear policies and procedures, including a comprehensive code of conduct and a transparent grievance process.

3. Training Programs: The company introduced regular training programs focused on communication, conflict resolution and leadership development.

4. Employee Involvement: Employees were involved in the decision-making process through regular feedback sessions and town hall meetings.

The Outcome

Within a year, the company saw a significant reduction in employee turnover and absenteeism. Employee engagement scores improved, and the overall workplace atmosphere became more positive and collaborative. The changes not only improved morale but also boosted productivity and client satisfaction.

Visualizing the Data

Employee Turnover Rates

A graph showing turnover rates before and after implementing anti-toxicity measures can illustrate the effectiveness of these initiatives. A downward trend in turnover rates indicates a positive impact.

Employee Satisfaction Scores

A chart comparing employee satisfaction scores over time can help visualize improvements in workplace culture. Higher satisfaction scores post-intervention suggest that the measures taken are working.

Conclusion

Identifying and addressing toxicity in the workplace is critical for creating a healthy, productive and engaging work environment. By recognizing the signs of toxicity, understanding its impact, and implementing best practices, organizations can foster a culture of respect, collaboration and well-being.

Creating a positive workplace is an ongoing process that requires commitment and effort from everyone in the organization. By prioritizing open communication, clear policies, regular training and active monitoring, we can build workplaces where employees feel valued, respected and motivated to contribute their best work.

Together, let's commit to identifying and eliminating toxicity in our workplaces, ensuring a brighter, more productive future for all.

Chapter 4

Identifying the Root Causes of Workplace Toxicity

Introduction

Before we can solve a problem, we need to understand it. Toxic workplaces don't just happen overnight. They develop over time, often due to a mix of poor management, weak policies and negative behaviours that go unchecked. In this chapter, we will explore the root causes of workplace toxicity. We will look at common factors that contribute to a toxic environment and how to identify them. Understanding these causes is essential for creating strategies to foster a healthier work culture.

Poor Leadership

Micromanagement

One of the most common causes of workplace toxicity is micromanagement. When leaders excessively control or monitor their employees, it undermines trust and autonomy. Employees feel stifled and undervalued, leading to decreased morale and productivity.

Example:

In a software development company, a manager insists on approving every line of code before it goes live. This level of control slows down the process and frustrates the team. Over time, developers become disengaged and less innovative.

Lack of Support

Leaders who fail to support their teams create a toxic environment. Support includes providing resources, guidance and recognition. Without it, employees feel abandoned and stressed.

Example:

A customer service team struggles with outdated software. Their manager is aware but does nothing to address the issue.

The team becomes frustrated and feels unsupported, leading to high employee turnover rates.

Ineffective Communication

Information Silos

When information is not shared freely, it creates barriers and fosters mistrust. Information silos occur when departments or individuals pile information, making it difficult for others to do their jobs effectively.

Example:

In a large corporation, the marketing and sales departments rarely communicate. Marketing launches campaigns without informing sales, leading to confusion and missed opportunities. This lack of coordination creates tension between the teams.

Poor Feedback Mechanisms

Feedback is crucial for growth and improvement. In toxic workplaces, feedback is often negative, unconstructive or absent. Employees don't know what they are doing right or wrong, leading to confusion and frustration.

Example:

An employee receives only critical feedback during annual reviews. They never hear about their successes or how they can improve constructively. This approach damages their confidence and engagement.

Unclear Expectations

When employees don't know what is expected of them, it creates uncertainty and stress. Clear expectations are essential for performance and job satisfaction.

Example:

A project manager assigns tasks without clear deadlines or deliverables. Team members are unsure of their priorities and timelines. This ambiguity leads to missed deadlines and frustration.

Unfair Treatment

Favouritism

Favouritism erodes trust and morale. When leaders consistently favour certain employees over others, it creates resentment and division within the team.

Example:

A manager consistently gives the most desirable projects to a select few employees. Others, who are equally capable, feel overlooked and undervalued. This favouritism breeds resentment and disengagement.

Discrimination and Harassment

Discrimination and harassment are severe forms of toxicity. They create a hostile work environment and can have legal consequences. Organizations must have strict policies and take immediate action against such behaviours.

Example:

An employee faces racial discrimination from a coworker. Despite reporting the issue, management takes no action. This inaction signals that such behaviour is tolerated, leading to a toxic culture.

Lack of Career Development

Employees need opportunities to grow and advance. When these opportunities are lacking, it leads to stagnation and disengagement.

Example:

A talented graphic designer feels stuck in their role with no clear path for advancement. Despite expressing interest in more challenging projects, they are consistently overlooked. This lack of development leads to frustration and eventual resignation.

Inadequate Work-Life Balance

Work-life balance is crucial for employee well-being. When employees are expected to work long hours or be available around the clock, it leads to burnout.

Example:

consulting firm expects employees to be available 24/7. This expectation creates immense stress and leads to high burnout rates. Employees struggle to maintain a healthy work-life balance and their personal lives suffer.

Real-World Case: M/s Wells Fargo Scandal

The Wells Fargo scandal is a prime example of how multiple toxic factors can converge. Employees were pressured to meet unrealistic sales targets, leading to fraudulent activities. Poor leadership, lack of support and unfair treatment created a toxic culture that ultimately led to significant legal and financial repercussions for the company.

https://en.wikipedia.org/wiki/Wells_Fargo_cross-selling_scandal

Best Practices for Addressing Root Causes

Establish Clear Communication Channels

Open and transparent communication is vital. Regular meetings, updates and feedback loops help ensure everyone is on the same page.

Example:

A tech startup holds weekly all-hands meetings where employees can ask questions and share updates. This practice promotes transparency and fosters a sense of community.

Set Clear Expectations

Clearly defined roles, responsibilities and goals help employees understand what is expected of them. Regular check-ins can help ensure alignment.

Example:

A marketing agency uses project management software to outline tasks, deadlines, and responsibilities. Employees know exactly what is expected and can track their progress.

Promote Fair Treatment

Ensure policies against favouritism, discrimination and harassment are strictly enforced. Training programs can help educate employees and leaders on these issues.

Example:

A financial firm implements mandatory diversity and inclusion training. They also establish a clear process for reporting and addressing complaints, ensuring all employees feel safe and valued.

Support Career Development

Invest in your employees' growth by providing training, mentorship and advancement opportunities.

Example:

A manufacturing company offers tuition reimbursement and internal training programs. Employees are encouraged to pursue further education and career development, leading to higher job satisfaction and retention.

Foster Work-Life Balance

Encourage a healthy work-life balance by setting realistic expectations and respecting employees' personal time. Flexible work schedules and remote work options can help.

Example:

A software development company introduces flexible working hours and the option to work from home. Employees report increased satisfaction and productivity as they can better manage their personal and professional lives.

Visualizing the Data

Visual aids can help highlight the root causes and effects of workplace toxicity. Here are some examples:

Causes of Workplace Toxicity

A chart can illustrate the most common causes of workplace toxicity based on employee surveys. For example, 30% might cite poor leadership, 25% ineffective communication, 20% unclear expectations, 15% unfair treatment, and 10% lack of career development.

Employee Turnover Rates

A graph comparing turnover rates in companies with toxic versus healthy cultures over several years can show the impact of toxicity. Toxic workplaces might see a steady increase in turnover rates, while healthy workplaces maintain stable or declining rates.

Productivity and Well-Being Metrics

A graph comparing productivity and well-being metrics before and after implementing changes to address toxicity can demonstrate the positive impact. For instance, after introducing clear communication channels and career development programs, productivity might increase by 20% and employee satisfaction by 25%.

Conclusion

Understanding the root causes of workplace toxicity is the first step toward creating a healthier, more productive work environment. By recognizing these causes and implementing best practices to address them, organizations can transform their cultures and improve the well-being and performance of their employees.

Creating a positive workplace is not just about avoiding the negative. It's about actively fostering an environment where employees feel valued, supported, and motivated. In the following chapters, we will explore practical strategies and real-world examples to help you implement these changes and build a thriving workplace.

Action Steps

1. Conduct an Internal Audit: Assess your workplace to identify the root causes of toxicity. Use surveys, interviews and observation to gather data.

2. Develop Clear Policies: Create and enforce policies that promote fair treatment, open communication and career development.

3. Train Leaders: Provide training for managers and leaders on effective leadership, communication and support strategies.

4. Monitor Progress: Regularly review and adjust your strategies based on feedback and performance metrics.

By taking these steps, you can begin to address the root causes of toxicity in your workplace and create a healthier, more supportive environment for all employees. Let's work together to build a better workplace where everyone can thrive.

Chapter 5

Strategies for Creating a Healthy Workplace Culture

Introduction

Creating a healthy workplace culture is not just a nice-to-have; it's a necessity for long-term success. A positive environment boosts morale, productivity and overall employee well-being. This chapter will explore the practical strategies to build and sustain a healthy workplace culture. We will cover actionable steps, real-world examples, and data to illustrate the benefits of a supportive work environment.

Building a Positive Culture from the Ground Up

Start with Core Values

Every company should have a clear set of core values that guide its culture. These values should reflect what the organization stands for and should be communicated clearly to all employees.

Example:

At a healthcare company, the core values include compassion, integrity and teamwork. These values are displayed prominently around the office and discussed regularly in meetings, ensuring everyone is aligned.

Encourage Open Communication

Open and honest communication is the cornerstone of a healthy workplace. Encourage employees to share their thoughts, ideas, and concerns without fear of retribution.

Example:

A tech startup holds monthly "town hall" meetings where employees can ask questions directly to the CEO. This practice fosters transparency and trust within the organization.

Creating a Supportive Environment

Promote Work-Life Balance

A healthy work-life balance is essential for employee well-being. Companies should encourage employees to take breaks, use their vacation days and set boundaries between work and personal life.

Examples:

1) A consulting firm implements a policy where emails are not expected to be answered after standard work hours or during the weekends. This policy helps employees disconnect and recharge, reducing burnout.

2) A manufacturing company implements a policy where the laptops are not allowed to be carried after standard work hours. If required, exceptional approval (with a business justification) is a must from the management.

Offer Professional Development Opportunities

Investing in employees' growth shows that the company values them. Provide opportunities for training, mentorship and career advancement.

Example:

A financial services company offers tuition reimbursement and internal training programs. Employees are encouraged to pursue further education and professional certifications, leading to higher job satisfaction and retention.

Recognize and Reward Achievements

Recognition is a powerful motivator. Regularly acknowledge and reward employees for their hard work and accomplishments.

Example:

A retail company has a monthly award for “Employee of the Month,” where the winner receives a bonus and public recognition. This practice boosts morale and encourages a positive work ethic.

Fostering a Collaborative Atmosphere

Build Strong Teams

Teamwork is essential for a healthy workplace. Encourage collaboration and create opportunities for team-building activities.

Example:

A marketing agency organizes quarterly team-building retreats where employees participate in workshops and activities designed to strengthen team cohesiveness. These retreats improve communication and collaboration back in the office.

Encourage Diversity and Inclusion

A diverse and inclusive workplace is a healthy one. Ensure that hiring practices promote diversity; and that all employees feel valued and included.

Example:

A software company creates an inclusion committee to oversee diversity initiatives. They conduct regular training sessions on unconscious bias and ensure all voices are heard in decision-making processes.

Implementing Health and Wellness Programs

Offer Wellness Programs

Wellness programs can significantly improve employee health and morale. These programs can include fitness classes, mental health resources and wellness challenges.

Example:

A manufacturing company provides on-site fitness classes and access to a mental health counsellor. Employees can attend yoga sessions during their breaks and have confidential consultations with the counsellor.

Create a Healthy Physical Environment

The physical work environment plays a vital role in employee well-being. Ensure the workplace is safe, comfortable and conducive to productivity.

Example:

A law firm upgrades its office space to include ergonomic furniture, natural lighting and quiet zones for focused work. These changes lead to reduced physical strain and enhanced job satisfaction.

Measuring and Sustaining a Healthy Culture

Regularly Assess Employee Satisfaction

Regular surveys and feedback sessions can help gauge employee satisfaction and identify areas for improvement. Use this data from surveys and feedback to make informed changes.

Example:

An insurance company conducts quarterly employee satisfaction surveys. The results are reviewed by management and actionable steps are taken to address any concerns raised by employees.

Monitor 'Key Performance Indicators' (KPIs)

Measure the success of your cultural initiatives through KPIs such as employee turnover rates, absenteeism and productivity levels.

Example:

A logistics firm tracks absenteeism rates before and after implementing a wellness program. They see a 15% decrease in absenteeism, indicating the program's positive impact.

Real-World Case: M/s CBA Positive Culture

M/s CBA, the outdoor apparel company, is renowned for its healthy workplace culture. The company promotes work-life balance, environmental activism and employee well-being. M/s CBA offers flexible work hours, on-site childcare and encourages employees to engage in environmental causes. This supportive culture has led to high employee satisfaction and loyalty, showcasing the benefits of a positive work environment.

Visualizing the Data

Employee Satisfaction

A graph comparing employee satisfaction scores before and after implementing cultural initiatives can highlight the impact of these changes. For instance, satisfaction scores might increase from 70% to 85%.

Employee Turnover Rates

A graph showing employee turnover rates over time can illustrate the effectiveness of creating a healthy culture. A decrease in turnover rates post-implementation can be a strong indicator of success.

Productivity Metrics

A chart depicting productivity metrics before and after cultural changes can show improvements in efficiency and output. For example, productivity might increase by 20% after introducing professional development programs.

Conclusion

Creating a healthy workplace culture requires commitment and effort, but the benefits are well worth it. By focusing on core values, open communication, support, collaboration and well-being, companies can build an environment where employees thrive. As we've seen from the examples and data, these strategies lead to ***happier, more productive employees and a stronger, more successful organization.***

The journey to a positive workplace culture is ongoing. Regular assessment and adaptation are key to sustaining a healthy environment. In the next chapters, we will explore deeper into specific strategies and tools that can help you continue to build and maintain a thriving workplace. Let's work together to create a culture where everyone feels valued, supported and empowered to do their best work.

Chapter 6

Implementing Effective Conflict Resolution Strategies

Introduction

Conflict in the workplace is inevitable. Whether it's a disagreement over project direction or a clash of personalities, conflicts can arise in any organization. However, how these conflicts are handled can significantly impact the work environment. In this chapter, we will explore effective conflict resolution strategies that foster a positive workplace culture. We will discuss practical steps, share real-world examples and present data to illustrate the importance of addressing conflicts constructively.

Understanding Workplace Conflict

Types of Conflict

Conflicts can be broadly categorized into several types, each requiring different approaches:

1. Task Conflict: Disagreements about the content and outcomes of tasks.

2. Relationship Conflict: Personal incompatibilities create tension and animosity.

3. Process Conflict: Disputes over how tasks should be completed.

Example:

In a marketing firm, team members argue about the direction of a new campaign (task conflict), while two colleagues clash over work styles (relationship conflict). Meanwhile, there's a disagreement on the project's timeline (process conflict).

Causes of Conflict

Understanding the root causes of conflict can help in resolving them more effectively. Common causes include:

1. *Communication Breakdown*: Misunderstandings or lack of information.

2. *Differing Goals and Priorities*: Misaligned objectives among team members.

3. *Resource Scarcity*: Limited resources lead to competition.

4. *Personality Clashes*: Differences in character and work styles.

Example:

A software development team faces conflict due to unclear communication from leadership, leading to confusion about project priorities.

Strategies for Effective Conflict Resolution

Open Communication

Encouraging open and honest communication can prevent many conflicts from escalating. Create an environment where employees feel safe to express their concerns.

Example:

A tech company implements regular “check-in” meetings where team members discuss any issues they face. This practice helps identify and address conflicts early.

Active Listening

Listening actively means paying full attention to the speaker, acknowledging their points and responding thoughtfully. It’s crucial to understand all perspectives in a conflict.

Example:

During a dispute about project roles, a manager listens to each team member’s concerns without interrupting. This approach helps clarify misunderstandings and find common ground.

Mediation and Facilitation

Sometimes, conflicts require a neutral third party to facilitate resolution. Mediation involves an impartial mediator helping the disputing parties find a mutually acceptable solution.

Example:

In a retail company, a mediator is brought in to resolve a conflict between the sales and marketing departments. The mediator helps them understand each other's perspectives and agree on a collaborative approach.

Developing Conflict Resolution Skills

Training Programs

Providing conflict resolution training can equip employees with the skills they need to manage disputes effectively. Training can include communication techniques, negotiation skills and problem-solving strategies.

Example:

A healthcare organization offers workshops on conflict management. Employees learn how to handle disagreements professionally, reducing workplace tension.

Role-Playing Exercises

Role-playing can be an effective way to practice conflict resolution in a safe environment. These exercises help employees prepare for real-life situations.

Example:

During a training session, employees at a manufacturing firm engage in role-playing scenarios. They practice resolving conflicts over resource allocation, improving their ability to handle similar issues on the job.

Creating a Conflict Resolution Policy

Clear Procedures

Establish clear procedures for addressing conflicts. Ensure all employees understand the steps to take when a conflict arises and whom to contact for assistance.

Example:

A finance company develops a conflict resolution policy outlining the process for reporting and addressing disputes. The policy includes steps for mediation and escalation if needed.

Confidentiality

Maintain confidentiality throughout the conflict resolution process to build trust and encourage employees to come forward with their concerns.

Example:

An advertising agency ensures that all conflict resolution discussions are confidential. This approach helps employees feel secure in voicing their issues without fear of retaliation.

Leveraging Data and Feedback

Monitoring Conflict Trends

Regularly collect and analyze data on workplace conflicts to identify patterns and areas needing improvement. Use this information to adjust policies and training programs.

Example:

A logistics firm tracks conflict incidents and discovers a high number of disputes in the warehouse. They implement targeted training and see a significant reduction in conflicts.

Employee Feedback

Encourage employees to provide feedback on the conflict resolution process. Use their insights to refine and improve your approach.

Example:

A consulting company conducts anonymous surveys to gather feedback on its conflict resolution procedures. Employees suggest improvements, leading to a more effective system.

Real-World Case: M/s XYZ's Conflict Management Approach

M/s XYZ, known for its innovative workplace culture, takes conflict resolution seriously. The company provides extensive training for managers and employees on handling conflicts. They also use data-driven approaches to monitor and address conflicts proactively. This commitment to conflict management has helped Google maintain a positive and productive work environment.

Visualizing the Data

Conflict Resolution Success Rate

A graph showing the success rate of conflict resolution efforts over time can highlight the effectiveness of your strategies. For instance, the graph might show a steady increase in resolved conflicts following the implementation of new strategies.

Employee Satisfaction

A chart comparing employee satisfaction scores before and after conflict resolution training can illustrate the positive impact of these initiatives. For example, satisfaction might increase by 15% post-training.

Conclusion

Effective conflict resolution is essential for maintaining a healthy workplace culture. By understanding the types and causes of conflict, fostering open communication and equipping employees with the necessary skills, organizations can manage disputes constructively. Clear policies and ongoing training are crucial for sustaining these efforts.

Addressing conflicts promptly and professionally not only resolves issues but also strengthens team dynamics and trust. In the next chapters, we will explore additional strategies and tools to further enhance your workplace culture. Together, we can build an environment where conflicts are seen not as obstacles but as opportunities for growth and improvement.

Chapter 7

Nurturing Employee Well-being for a Thriving Workplace

Introduction

Employee well-being is not just a buzzword; it's the foundation of a thriving workplace. When employees feel valued, supported and healthy, they perform at their best, driving organizational success. In this chapter, we will delve into strategies for nurturing employee well-being, exploring practical approaches, real-world examples and data to illustrate the importance of prioritizing the health and happiness of your workforce.

Understanding Employee Well-being

What is Employee Well-being?

Employee well-being encompasses physical, mental, and emotional health, as well as overall satisfaction and engagement at work. It's about creating an environment where employees can thrive both personally and professionally.

Example:

An employee who feels physically energized, mentally stimulated and emotionally supported at work is likely experiencing high levels of well-being.

The Impact of Employee Well-being

Investing in employee well-being yields numerous benefits for organizations, including:

1. *Increased Productivity*: Healthy and happy employees are more focused and motivated, leading to higher productivity levels.

2. *Improved Employee Retention*: When employees feel valued and supported, they are more likely to stay with the company long-term.

3. *Enhanced Engagement*: Engaged employees are emotionally invested in their work and go above and beyond to contribute to the organization's success.

Data: According to a study by Gallup, highly engaged teams show 21% greater profitability.

Strategies for Nurturing Employee Well-being

Promoting Work-Life Balance

Encourage employees to maintain a healthy balance between their work responsibilities and personal lives. Provide flexible work arrangements, encourage the use of vacation time and discourage overtime work.

Example:

A technology company implements a "work from anywhere" policy, allowing employees to choose where they work based on their preferences and needs. This flexibility helps employees manage their work-life balance more effectively.

Prioritizing Mental Health Support

Mental health is a critical component of overall well-being. Offer resources and support for employees experiencing stress, anxiety or other mental health challenges. This can include access to counselling services, mindfulness programs and mental health awareness training.

Example:

A financial institution partners with a local mental health organization to provide confidential counselling services for employees. Additionally, they offer workshops on stress management and resilience-building techniques.

Encouraging Physical Activity

Regular physical activity is essential for maintaining good physical and mental health. Encourage employees to incorporate movement into their daily routines through initiatives such as walking meetings, on-site fitness classes or wellness challenges.

Example:

A manufacturing company installs standing desks and encourages employees to take regular walking breaks throughout the day. They also organize weekly yoga sessions to promote relaxation and flexibility.

Fostering a Positive Work Environment

Create a supportive and inclusive work environment where employees feel valued, respected and appreciated. Recognize and celebrate achievements, encourage collaboration and address issues such as bullying or harassment promptly and effectively.

Example:

A hospitality company implements a peer recognition program where employees can nominate their colleagues for outstanding performance. This program helps foster a culture of appreciation and support within the organization.

Providing Opportunities for Growth and Development

Invest in employees' professional growth and development to help them reach their full potential. Offer training programs, mentorship opportunities and career advancement paths to empower employees to achieve their career goals.

Example:

A healthcare organization offers tuition reimbursement for employees pursuing further education or professional certifications. They also provide access to leadership development programs to help employees advance within the company.

Measuring and Monitoring Employee Well-being

Employee Surveys

Regularly survey employees to assess their satisfaction and well-being levels. Ask questions about work-life balance, job satisfaction, stress levels and support resources to identify areas for improvement.

Example:

A retail company conducts quarterly employee satisfaction surveys, including questions related to work-life balance and stress levels. They use the survey results to inform their well-being initiatives and track progress over time.

Absenteeism and Employee Turnover Rates

Monitor absenteeism and employee turnover rates as indicators of employee well-being. High levels of absenteeism or employee turnover may signal underlying issues with work-related stress, job satisfaction, or organizational culture.

Data: According to the Society for Human Resource Management (SHRM), the average cost of employee turnover is between 50% and 60% of an employee's annual salary.

Real-World Case: Airbnb's Focus on Employee Well-being

Airbnb, the global hospitality company, is known for its commitment to employee well-being. The company offers a range of well-being programs, including meditation classes, wellness reimbursements and flexible work arrangements. Airbnb also prioritizes mental health support, providing access to counselling services and mental health resources for employees. This focus on well-being has contributed to high levels of employee satisfaction and retention at Airbnb. https://news.airbnb.com/airbnbs-design-to-live-and-work-anywhere/

Visualizing the Data

Employee Satisfaction Ratings

A graph tracking employee satisfaction ratings over time can illustrate trends in employee well-being. For example, an upward trend in satisfaction ratings may indicate the success of well-being initiatives implemented by the organization.

Absenteeism Trends

A chart comparing absenteeism rates before and after the implementation of well-being programs can demonstrate their impact on employee attendance. A decrease in absenteeism rates following the introduction of these programs indicates improved employee well-being.

Conclusion

Nurturing employee well-being is essential for creating a thriving workplace where employees can perform at their best. By prioritizing work-life balance, mental health support, physical activity, a positive work environment and opportunities for growth and development, organizations can create a culture that values and supports its employees' well-being.

Measuring and monitoring employee well-being through surveys, absenteeism rates and turnover rates allows organizations to track progress and make data-driven decisions to further enhance well-being initiatives.

In the next chapters, we will explore additional strategies and best practices for cultivating a healthy and supportive workplace culture. Together, let's create an environment where employees can thrive and contribute to the success of the organization.

Chapter 8

Cultivating Diversity and Inclusion in the Workplace

Introduction

Diversity and inclusion are not just buzzwords; they are fundamental pillars of a successful and thriving workplace. Embracing diversity means recognizing and valuing differences among employees, while inclusion ensures that everyone feels welcome, respected and able to contribute their unique perspectives. In this chapter, we will explore the importance of cultivating diversity and inclusion in the workplace, along with practical strategies, real-world examples and data to illustrate the benefits of embracing diversity and fostering an inclusive culture.

Understanding Diversity and Inclusion

What is Diversity?

Diversity refers to the range of differences among individuals in a workplace, including but not limited to race, ethnicity, gender, age, sexual orientation, disability, religion and socioeconomic background.

Example:

A diverse workforce may include employees from various cultural backgrounds, generations and experiences, bringing a collage of perspectives and ideas to the table.

What is Inclusion?

Inclusion is about creating an environment where every individual feels valued, respected and included, regardless of their differences. It involves fostering a sense of belonging and ensuring that all employees have equal opportunities to thrive.

Example:

An inclusive workplace promotes collaboration, openness and mutual respect, enabling employees to fully participate and contribute to the organization's success.

The Benefits of Diversity and Inclusion

Enhanced Innovation and Creativity

A diverse workforce brings together people with different backgrounds, experiences, and perspectives, sparking creativity and innovation. By encouraging diverse viewpoints, organizations can develop more innovative solutions to challenges.

Data: According to a study by McKinsey, companies in the top quartile for gender diversity are 15% more likely to have financial returns above their respective national industry medians.

https://www.mckinsey.com/~/media/McKinsey/Email/Classics/2020/2020-02-classic.html#:~:text=The%20moral%20case%20for%20workforce,for%20gender%20diversity%2C%2015%20percent.

Improved Decision-Making

Diverse teams are better equipped to consider a wide range of perspectives and insights, leading to more informed and effective decision-making. By leveraging diverse viewpoints, organizations can make better decisions that reflect the needs and preferences of their diverse customer base.

Example:

A technology company forms a cross-functional team with members from different departments and backgrounds to brainstorm ideas for a new product launch. The diverse team's discussions lead to innovative features and marketing strategies that resonate with a broader audience.

Increased Employee Engagement and Satisfaction

Employees who feel included and valued are more engaged, motivated and satisfied with their work. Inclusive workplaces foster a sense of belonging and loyalty among employees, leading to higher retention rates and productivity.

Data: A study by Deloitte found that inclusive teams are 10 times more likely to be highly effective and nine times more likely to innovate.

https://www2.deloitte.com/content/dam/insights/us/articles/4209_Diversity-and-inclusion-revolution/DI_Diversity-and-inclusion-revolution.pdf

Strategies for Cultivating Diversity and Inclusion

Leadership Commitment and Accountability

Leadership plays a crucial role in driving diversity and inclusion initiatives. Leaders should demonstrate a commitment to diversity and inclusion through their actions, decisions and behaviours. They should hold themselves and others accountable for creating an inclusive culture.

Example:

The CEO of a financial services firm publicly commits to diversity and inclusion goals and holds regular meetings with senior leadership to review progress and address any barriers to inclusion.

Diverse Hiring Practices

Implementing diverse hiring practices is essential for building a diverse workforce. This includes sourcing candidates from a wide range of backgrounds, using blind recruitment techniques to reduce bias and ensuring diverse representation on hiring panels.

Example:

A healthcare organization partners with community organizations to recruit candidates from underrepresented groups. They also implement blind resume screening to ensure candidates are evaluated based on their qualifications rather than demographic information.

Inclusive Policies and Practices

Review and update organizational policies and practices to ensure they promote diversity and inclusion. This includes policies related to recruitment, promotion, training and development and employee benefits.

Example:

A retail company in the US has revised its parental leave policy to be more inclusive of all types of families, including adoptive parents and same-sex couples. They also offer flexible work arrangements to accommodate employees' diverse needs.

Diversity Training and Education

Provide training and education programs to raise awareness of diversity and inclusion issues and equip employees with the skills to create an inclusive workplace. Training topics may include unconscious bias, cultural competence and allyship.

Example:

An engineering firm offers workshops on unconscious bias and inclusive leadership for all employees. They also provide resources and support for employees to become diversity and inclusion ambassadors within their teams.

Measuring and Monitoring Diversity and Inclusion

Diversity Metrics

Track diversity metrics such as representation rates, turnover rates and promotion rates by demographic group to assess progress and identify areas for improvement.

Data: According to a study by Harvard Business Review, companies with diverse management teams have 19% higher revenue due to innovation.

https://www.forbes.com/sites/annapowers/2018/06/27/a-study-finds-that-diverse-companies-produce-19-more-revenue/?sh=79d9583a506f

Employee Feedback and Surveys

Regularly solicit feedback from employees through surveys and focus groups to gauge perceptions of diversity and inclusion within the organization. Use this feedback to inform decision-making and prioritize areas for action.

Example:

A technology company conducts an annual diversity and inclusion survey to gather feedback from employees. The survey results are analysed and action plans are developed to address any concerns raised by employees.

Real-World Case: Salesforce's cutting-edge Diversity Initiatives

Salesforce, a leading cloud-based software company, is known for its cutting-edge diversity and inclusion initiatives. The company has set ambitious diversity goals, including achieving gender pay equity and increasing the representation of underrepresented groups in leadership positions. Salesforce also offers extensive diversity training programs and resources for employees and has created employee resource groups to support diverse communities within the organization.

Visualizing the Data

Diversity Representation

A chart showing the demographic breakdown of employees by race, gender, age and other characteristics can provide a snapshot of diversity within the organization. This visual representation can help identify areas where representation may be lacking.

Employee Satisfaction Ratings

A graph tracking employee satisfaction ratings over time, broken down by demographic group, can illustrate disparities in satisfaction levels and identify potential areas for improvement in inclusion efforts.

Conclusion

Cultivating diversity and inclusion in the workplace is not just the right thing to do; it's also essential for driving innovation, improving decision-making and fostering employee engagement and satisfaction. By implementing strategies such as leadership commitment, diverse hiring practices, inclusive policies and ongoing measurement and monitoring, organizations can create a culture where every employee feels valued, respected and empowered to contribute their best work.

Together, let's strive to create environments where diversity is celebrated and inclusion is the norm.

Conclusion

Building a Better Workplace Together

Creating a positive and productive workplace is not just a goal; it's an ongoing journey that requires dedication, commitment and collaboration from everyone involved. Throughout this book, we have explored various aspects of fostering a healthy workplace culture, from addressing toxicity and conflict to nurturing employee well-being and embracing diversity and inclusion. As we conclude our journey, let's reflect on the key takeaways and the path forward to building a better workplace together.

Recognizing the Importance of Workplace Culture

Workplace culture is the heartbeat of any organization, shaping its values, behaviours and overall environment. A positive culture fosters collaboration, innovation and employee engagement, while a toxic culture can lead to disengagement, employee turnover and decreased productivity. By recognizing the impact of culture on organizational success, we can take proactive steps to cultivate a culture that brings out the best in everyone.

Addressing Toxicity and Conflict

Toxicity and conflict are inevitable in any workplace, but how we address them can make all the difference. By identifying the root causes of toxicity and implementing effective conflict resolution strategies, we can create a healthier and more harmonious work environment. Encouraging open communication, active listening and mediation can help resolve conflicts constructively and prevent them from escalating.

Nurturing Employee Well-being

Employee well-being is essential for both individual fulfillment and organizational success. By prioritizing work-life balance, mental health support, physical activity and a positive work environment, we can create conditions where employees can thrive personally and professionally. Investing in employee well-being not only enhances productivity and engagement but also fosters a culture of care and compassion within the organization.

Embracing Diversity and Inclusion

Diversity and inclusion are not just buzzwords; they are fundamental principles that drive innovation, creativity and organizational resilience. By embracing diversity and fostering an inclusive culture, we can harness the power of different perspectives and experiences to solve complex problems and achieve shared goals. Through diverse hiring practices, inclusive policies, and ongoing education and training, we can create a workplace where everyone feels valued, respected and empowered to succeed.

The Path Forward

As we conclude our exploration of building a better workplace, let us commit to taking action and making positive changes within our organizations. By implementing the strategies and best practices discussed in this book, ***we can create environments where employees feel supported, motivated and inspired to do their best work.*** Let's continue to listen to our employees, adapt to changing needs and strive for continuous improvement in all aspects of workplace culture.

Real-World Examples

Throughout this book, we have seen real-world examples of organizations that have successfully implemented strategies to improve workplace culture. From a company that focuses on employee well-being to another company where a commitment to diversity and inclusion, these examples serve as inspiration and proof that positive change is possible. By learning from these success stories and adapting them to our own contexts, we can create workplaces where everyone can thrive.

Visualizing Success

Visual aids such as data charts, graphs and pictorial presentations have helped us understand the impact of workplace culture initiatives and track progress over time. By visualizing success through metrics such as employee satisfaction ratings, diversity representation and turnover rates, we can identify areas for improvement and measure the effectiveness of our efforts. Let's continue to use data-driven insights to guide our decision-making and ensure that our initiatives have a meaningful impact on workplace culture.

Conclusion: A Call to Action

As we conclude our journey of exploring workplace culture, let us remember that building a better workplace is a collective effort that requires commitment, empathy and continuous learning. Let's commit to creating environments where everyone feels valued, respected and empowered to contribute their best work. By fostering a culture of trust, collaboration and inclusion, we can create workplaces that not only drive organizational success but also enrich the lives of all who are part of them. Together, let's build a great workplace for today and carry the legacy of a great workplace for generations to come.

At the end let me say

Some of these strategies/successful practices you may have read or come across before.

But here's the deal: Your life won't change until your HABITS and PRACTICES change.

Merely reading or consuming success material doesn't change your life. I would encourage you to select your requisite strategy from this book and implement it in your daily life/organisation IMMEDIATELY.

Slowly but surely, you will begin to achieve things you never thought would have been possible...

If you liked this book, do consider leaving a review on Amazon. It only takes a few minutes but would help and motivate me to write more books.

I recommend you also read my other publications, titled

1. "Build a High-Performance Culture"

2. "High-Productivity Practices – From Successful Leaders – A Road to Success"

3. "What Great Managers Do Differently – Unlocking the Secrets of Extraordinary Leadership and Management"

which are available on www.amazon.com / www.hroptimum.com

For other reading materials on HR management, please visit my blog page: https://hroptimum.com/blog

Your suggestions and feedback would be most welcome. You may kindly do so at: coach.drravindran@gmail.com

Thank you so much!

Happy Reading! Keep Reading and grow steadily.

About the Author

The Author Dr.Ravindran.K.A. (Bachelor of Commerce [B. Com], Bachelor of Laws [LL. B), Masters in Personnel Management & Industrial Relations [M.A. – PM&IR.] and a Ph.D. holder in Management is a seasoned Human Resource Management professional with three decades of hands-on work experience in various industries, majorly well-known Japanese Corporates, managing the entire Human Resource & General Affairs functions in senior leadership roles. Throughout his corporate journey, he has helped many lives within organizations to reach their career aspirations through effective coaching and mentoring. Outside the organization also, the HR fraternity members are being supported, and they have been consulting him for effective people management practices. He has closely experienced the challenges people face in organizations, and he has provided them with workable solutions to help them overcome those challenges from time to time as required.

Dr. Ravindran has many publications to his credit in various journals, newspapers, and newsletters on topics related to Human Resource Management. Also, he has published his first book titled “Build A High-Performance Culture” which has become a bestseller on Amazon and subsequently two more books titled “High-Productivity Practices – From Successful Leaders – A Road to Success” and "What Great Managers Do Differently"

Dr. Ravindran lives in New Delhi, India, with his wife, Mrs. Preethi Ravindran, daughter Ms. Ananya Ravindran and son Mr. Ananjay Ravindran.

www.ingramcontent.com/pod-product-compliance
Ingram Content Group UK Ltd.
Pitfield, Milton Keynes, MK11 3LW, UK
UKHW041348190726
13845UKWH00026B/478

9 789314 100293